HOW TO TAME A

FUCK BOY

12 Steps for Taming Your Fuck Boy

Emmanuel Simms

In Vivo Exposure LLC

HOW TO TAME A F*CK BOY

12 Steps for Taming Your Fuck Boy

By

Emmanuel Simms

DEDICATION

To all the people I've unintentionally hurt in my past,

Unknowingly, I was a GPSMF. The realization
was slow, the healing even slower. I sincerely
hope you are well and find your peace.

May this journey offer both an understanding and an
olive branch to the times we faltered, the hearts that were
fractured, and the lessons that eventually led to clarity.

In growth, in reflection, and with hope for a brighter tomorrow.

INTRODUCTION: THE GPSMF PHENOMENON: UNDERSTANDING THE MODERN RELATIONSHIP MAZE

Before We Dive In... The Definition Detour

As we embark on this voyage to comprehend and, perhaps, tame the ever-elusive 'fuck boy', it's crucial we're equipped with the right lexicon. But this isn't just a cheeky term. We've taken a deep dive, blended it with scholarly flair, and emerged with a mental health diagnosis. (Surprising, isn't it?)

Introducing...

GPSMF: Grandiose Philanderer Shittart Mother Fucker

Each word isn't merely for comedic effect but intricately tied to behavioral attributes:

Grandiose: Reflecting the oversized confidence and exaggerated sense of self-importance.

Philanderer: Denoting the habitual pattern of pursuing romantic adventures, often without commitment.

Shittart: A nod to the complex choreography of charm and chaos they weave seamlessly.

Mother Fucker: For those moments when they leave us staggered, torn between exasperation and a begrudging admiration.

While GPSMF may seem reminiscent of GPS Mother Fucker, especially with their innate prowess to lead us into emotional mazes, the term offers a profound diagnostic insight.

You see, during my rigorous years in grad school, studying the intricacies of mental health, a light bulb flashed. The 'fuck boy' isn't a mythical creature from modern dating folklore; it's a product of specific environments. Societal, familial, and peer influences shape and mold this genderless entity, resulting in the character we're all too familiar with. This realization transformed GPSMF from a humorous epithet to a serious contender for inclusion in the annals of psychiatric nomenclature.

Word on the academic streets hints at its possible acknowledgment in the upcoming DSM-6 diagnostic manual. Far-fetched? Maybe. But when you reflect on the impacts and intricacies of GPSMF behavior, it's not as outlandish as it might initially appear.

As we navigate the chapters ahead, remember: understanding is the first step to compassion. And if you find yourself irresistibly drawn to assist these characters, let this book be your guiding star. Ah, the modern age—a glorious time of technological marvels, alternative milks, and... GPSMFs? If you've picked up this book, you either have an unhealthy obsession with unfamiliar acronyms or you're entangled in the chaotic web of a Grandiose Philanderer Shittart Mother F**ker (GPSMF for short, because let's face it, that's quite a mouthful).

Welcome, brave soul. Your relationship journey might've been a little bumpier than most, filled with more twists and turns than a reality TV show, but fear not. This guide is your roadmap through the maze, sprinkled with a healthy dose of humor because sometimes, if you don't laugh, you'll cry. Or throw things. Both are frowned upon in most public settings.

Now, what is this GPSMF phenomenon, you ask? Picture this: a suave, charming individual who sweeps you off your feet, only to drop you when the next shiny thing comes along. Sounds familiar? Well, you're not alone. In this book, we'll explore the complexities of taming (or coming to terms with) the ubiquitous GPSMF that's wormed their way into your heart.

But first, a little backstory. How did we land in this GPSMF-infested relationship landscape? Perhaps it's the influence of swipe-right culture, where options are plenty, and attention spans are, well, not. Or maybe it's the tantalizing allure of the "bad boy" or "wild girl" trope, propagated by movies where the protagonist magically "fixes" their love interest by the end credits. Spoiler alert: Real life doesn't come with a script.

"Why This Book?" you wonder aloud, or perhaps internally if you're surrounded by potentially judgmental pets. Because amidst the myriad of relationship advice books promising moonlit walks and conflict-free conversations, there's a need for something real, raw, and relatable. A guide that acknowledges the messiness of modern love, yet offers actionable advice (and a few laughs) to navigate it.

So, whether you're a seasoned GPSMF magnet or just dipping your toes into the chaotic waters of modern romance, strap in. This journey is part self-discovery, part relationship navigation, and wholly entertaining.

Let's dive in, shall we?

STEP 1
ADMITTING

Recognizing The GPSMF in Your Life

Just like every other 12-step program, the first step is admitting. Admitting that you have, well, a fuckboy that you happen to be head over heels for. Yes, you read that right. And there's nothing you can do about those fluttering heartbeats or that weird stomach flip every time they text. Any seasoned "Fuckboy Tamer" or long-suffering married individual will tell you there are only two ways to handle a fuckboy. One, pack your bags and hit the road, or two, what most well-intentioned but potentially misguided souls try to do: tame them. They believe if they shower them with love, understanding, and the occasional baked goods, the transformation from fuckboy to faithful partner will magically happen.

Error! System not supported. That way, my friend, often leads to heartbreak. And, if you're brave (or optimistic) enough to put a ring on it, a divorce could occur anywhere between six months to six years. Trust me; it happens more often than you'd think.

Now, if you picked up this book, you either found the title a cheeky delight or are genuinely seeking solace and wisdom on how to navigate this challenging relationship terrain. After all, the heart wants what it wants. It's stubborn like that. This book isn't here to chastise or judge. Whether you're a bro, sis, or anywhere in between, dealing with a fuckboy is no walk in the park. Love is real, palpable, and powerful. It's as genuine as mental health issues and sometimes just as complex. Like any other addictive behavior that folks want help to coexist with, there's often a 12-step program. So, welcome to ours.

Now, let's clarify something vital: labeling someone a 'fuckboy' doesn't immediately brand them as the villain in your personal rom-com. I feel for fuckboys; truly, I do. Especially because being one often isn't a conscious choice—at least, not initially. Being a fuckboy only solidifies as a lifestyle choice if one continues to be one post their "aha" moment of self-awareness. Will they admit it? Not likely. A true-blue fuckboy would rather claim they've seen a unicorn than confess their ways, and a reformed one? Well, they'd dodge the topic, but mainly out of lingering guilt.

But let's not throw a pity party for these behaviors. The mission here is to empower *you*. To help you understand yourself first and then the charming enigma you're dealing with. A quick PSA: this book isn't a replacement for professional counseling or therapy. If you feel you're in over your head, there's no shame in seeking professional help. There are plenty of fantastic programs and counselors out there.

The 'Aha' Moment: Recognizing You've Got a GPSMF

It's a sunny afternoon, birds are chirping, your latte is the right amount of foamy, and suddenly it hits you. The charming prince or princess you've been daydreaming about, telling your friends about, and probably dedicating Taylor Swift songs to, might just be a GPSMF. Cue dramatic gasp!

It starts subtly: maybe a little white lie about where they were last Friday, or that strangely intimate "friendship" with someone they swore was just a "study buddy". It's like assembling a jigsaw puzzle with a few pieces that just... don't fit.

You start to notice other things, too. They're always late, or they cancel plans at the last minute. They're always talking about themselves, and they never seem to ask you about your life. You start to feel like you're walking on eggshells around them, and you're always trying to please them.

And then, one day, you have the 'aha' moment. You realize that you're not in a healthy relationship. You're with someone who is constantly lying to you, manipulating you, and taking advantage of you. You're with a GPSMF.

It's a tough realization to come to, but it's the first step towards getting out of a toxic relationship. Once you realize what's going on, you can start to take steps to protect yourself. You can set boundaries, you can stop making excuses for their behavior, and you can start to move on with your life.

It's not easy, but it's worth it. You deserve to be in a relationship with someone who loves and respects you. You deserve to be with someone who is honest with you, who is reliable, and who makes you feel good about yourself.

So if you think you might be in a relationship with a GPSMF, don't be afraid to reach out for help. There are people who care about you and who want to help you get out of this situation. You can do this.

From Hollywood to Reality

Rom-coms often depict love and relationships in a very idealistic way. The couple usually overcomes all obstacles and ends up together, living happily ever after. However, in real life, things are not always so simple. Sometimes, the bad boy does not change his ways after the credits roll. In fact, he may even revert to his old habits. This can be a difficult thing to accept, especially if you are in love with the bad boy.

If you are in a relationship with a bad boy, it is important to remember that you deserve to be with someone who will treat you well and respect you. If the bad boy is not willing to do that, then you need to move on. It is not easy to admit that you are head over heels for a bad boy, but it is the first step to clarity. You need to take off those rose-tinted glasses and see your relationship for what it is: a challenge, a learning curve, and sometimes, a downright sitcom.

If you are willing to put in the work, then there is a chance that you can make things work with the bad boy. However, it is important to be realistic about your expectations. The bad boy may never change his ways completely. But if you are willing to accept him for who he is, then you may be able to have a happy and fulfilling relationship.

Ultimately, the decision of whether or not to stay with a bad boy is up to you. There is no right or wrong answer. Just make sure that you are making the decision for yourself, and not because you think it is what you are supposed to do.

The Many Faces of GPSMFs

Here's a plot twist: GPSMFs aren't one-size-fits-all. They come in all shapes, sizes, and genres. From the Casanova charmer to the commitment-phobe, from the breadcrumbing expert to the ghoster, the GPSMF kingdom is diverse and expansive.

But Why Admitting?

Because, dear reader, recognition is the precursor to action. Until we acknowledge the GPSMF in our lives, we're like hamsters on a wheel - running in circles, wondering why we aren't getting anywhere.

Admitting isn't just about labeling your partner. It's a mirror reflecting our choices, our patterns, and sometimes, our masochistic tendencies for drama. It's acknowledging that perhaps, we're addicted to the roller-coaster thrill, the uncertainty, the 'will they-won't they' dance.

Anecdote Alley: My GPSMF Rendezvous

The 'Surprise' Roommate

Lucy was head over heels in love with Dave, a suave guitarist with a penchant for late-night poetry. After a whirlwind three months, he mentioned he was looking for a place. Lucy, in her love-induced haze, offered him her spare room. One week turned into two, and soon Dave's "bandmates" were over every other night, turning her peaceful abode into a 24/7 jamming studio. And who never saw a cent for rent or those mysteriously disappearing snacks? Lucy. Every time she tried to broach the subject, Dave played the "working on our big break" card, and would serenade her into submission. It wasn't until Lucy came home to find Dave giving 'guitar lessons' to a suspiciously giggly blonde that she realized: her generous offer had turned her into the landlord of a Grade-A GPSMF, or Guy Playing Someone Else's Money.

Lucy was a kind and generous person, and she had always been willing to help others in need. But when she met Dave, she was blinded by love and didn't see the red flags that were right in front of her. Dave was a moocher and a user, and he took advantage of Lucy's kindness. He never paid rent, he ate her food, and he even brought his bandmates over to practice in her apartment. When Lucy finally confronted him about it, he just played the victim and said that he was "working on his big break." Lucy was heartbroken, but she knew that she had to kick Dave out of her apartment. She was tired of being taken advantage of, and she deserved better.

Lucy learned a valuable lesson from this experience: it's important to be careful who you let into your life. Just because someone is charming and says all the right things doesn't mean that they're a good person. It's important to trust your gut instinct and to not be afraid to stand up for yourself.

The Text Ghost

Sarah and Jake had an electric first date. Dinners, movies, late-night phone calls – it was textbook perfect. However, there was a catch. Every time Sarah tried to pin down a plan, Jake was mysteriously MIA, only to pop up with an 'adorably' apologetic text hours, or sometimes days later. He'd always have wild stories: abducted by aliens, helping a mysterious woman give birth in an elevator, or a sudden business trip to the Bermuda Triangle. Sarah, being the understanding partner, chuckled it off at first. It wasn't until she received a postcard, supposedly from Antarctica, with the words, "Sorry, got caught up with penguin business. TTYL!" that she recognized she'd been entertaining a GPSMF with a flair for the dramatic.

The Forgetful Romeo

Then there's Tom. Tom was the Romeo every Juliet dreamed of - roses on Tuesdays, surprise picnics, and moonlit boat rides. The works! Rita was floating on cloud nine, up until the day she received a beautiful bouquet with a card that read: "To Rachel, With all my love, Tom." As it turned out, Tom had several Juliets and had mixed up his deliveries. Rita was heartbroken, of course, but also slightly impressed at Tom's (mis)management skills. Who knew GPSMFs could be so resourcefully romantic?

Coming to Terms and Moving Forward

By the end of this chapter, if you've identified with even a fraction of the GPSMF tales, give yourself a pat on the back. The heart wants what it wants, but the mind? The mind is now informed. And as we tread this path together, remember: acknowledging the GPSMF is half the battle.

To be continued... in the maze of modern relationships!

STEP 2

BELIEVING

From Fairytale Dreams to Reality Checks: Trusting in Potential Change

Let's face it; everyone loves a fairytale. The whole premise of "Beauty and the Beast" is that with enough love and patience, even the wildest of beasts can be tamed. But life isn't a Disney movie, and GPSMFs aren't furry creatures hiding a princely heart beneath. When involved with a GPSMF, it's tempting to wrap oneself in the cocoon of 'potential' – believing that underneath those red flags lies a heart of gold just waiting to be discovered. However, it's essential to differentiate between genuine growth potential and the shimmering mirage of a transformation that's never going to happen.

Golden Nugget: Always remember, you are not a therapist (unless you are, then...different book). It's not your job to fix someone. Believe in their potential, but ensure it's grounded in reality and not just in your hopes.

Self-worth in the World of GPSMFs

It's easy to lose oneself in the turbulent tides of a GPSMF relationship. The highs are ecstatic, and the lows? Well, they can feel like the abyss. When you're constantly dealing with unpredictability, it can erode your self-worth.

But here's the deal: You're worthy. Your worth isn't determined by how many hoops you can jump through for someone or how many GPSMF tantrums you can tolerate. And most importantly, your value is not up for negotiation. Before you can truly believe in someone else's potential, you have to believe in your own worth first.

Golden Nugget: If you wouldn't accept certain behaviors from a friend, don't accept them from a partner. Period.

When Belief Takes a Comical Turn

Oh, the things we've believed!

1. The Dietary Restrictions:
Meet Bella. She believed when her GPSMF, Max, said he couldn't respond to her texts promptly because he had recently adopted a strict vegan diet which affected his texting fingers' agility. Yep, you heard that right. And she only questioned it when he texted swiftly for pizza delivery.

2. The Midnight Yoga:
Daniel always seemed to disappear during late-night hours, citing an exclusive 'midnight yoga' club that was helping him "find his center". It was all Zen until his roommate innocently asked why he was always at the local bar and never at yoga.

3. The Tech Guru:
Lila's GPSMF, Toby, once explained his inability to pick up calls by claiming he was beta testing a new tech feature for a giant tech company where calls "just didn't work" on his phone. This excuse was entertaining until she spotted him FaceTiming at a cafe.

Belief, when rooted in reality and self-worth, is a powerful tool. It becomes the foundation upon which you can build a healthy relationship or realize that perhaps the skyscraper you're imagining is better suited as a quaint, one-story house. Either way, it starts with believing in yourself.

Remember, as we navigate the world of GPSMFs, it's vital to strike a balance between optimism, realism, and a good dose of humor. After all, if we can't laugh at the absurdities, what's the point?

Belief Barometer: Navigating the Gray Zone

When it comes to matters of the heart, few things are ever black and white. Most of us reside in the expansive, often confusing gray zone, especially when GPSMFs (FuckBoys) are involved. This is why we've crafted the *Belief Barometer*, a lighthearted yet enlightening tool designed to help you understand where your belief levels stand.

◆◆ **Instructions:** For each statement below, rate how often it applies to your relationship on a scale from 1 to 5. 1 means "Rarely" and 5 means "All the time."

1. Even though there are red flags, I believe they're just temporary challenges.

2. I've envisioned our perfect future together more than I've thought about our present.

3. Friends and family constantly ask if I'm sure about my GPSMF, but I confidently brush off their concerns.

4. I often find myself justifying my GPSMF's actions, even when I don't fully understand them myself.

5. Deep down, I believe that if I show enough patience and understanding, my GPSMF will eventually see things my way.

6. Whenever things go south, I remind myself of that one perfect moment, week, or month as proof that things will get better.

7. I've invested more in self-help books and relationship advice

columns in the last year than ever before.

8. I believe that my GPSMF has the potential to change, even if they've shown no real signs of wanting to.

9. Whenever I think about leaving, a small part of me fears I might be giving up on the "best thing" that ever happened to me.

10. My gut occasionally tells me to be cautious, but my heart always wins the argument.

RESULTS:

- **10-20: Healthy Optimism** - You acknowledge the issues but believe in the relationship's potential. You're grounded in reality but optimistic about the future.

- **21-30: Hopeful Romantic** - You're a dreamer, and while that's not always bad, it's essential to ensure you're not ignoring some glaring issues.

- **31-40: Rose-tinted Realist** - You're starting to wade deep into the gray zone. It might be time to take a step back and reassess.

- **41-50: Delusional Dreamer** - Hope is essential, but remember, belief without evidence or mutual effort can lead to heartache. Seek balance and perhaps even external counsel.

The *Belief Barometer* isn't definitive, nor is it a substitute for professional advice. Instead, view it as a playful reflection tool, nudging you to consider just how much 'belief' you're investing and where it's leading you in the maze of GPSMF relationships.

Retro Reflections: Famous GPSMFs Throughout History

Imagine Cleopatra telling Julius Caesar he's been MIA because of a chariot malfunction or Romeo texting Juliet that he can't make it to their secret rendezvous due to a surprise

Capulet family dinner. This section offers a humorous look at how historical figures might have dealt with their own GPSMF situations, drawing parallels to modern-day GPSMF escapades and showcasing that believing in 'potential' isn't a new phenomenon.

Belief Boosters: Affirmations for the GPSMF Weary

Sometimes, we just need a little pep talk. This section offers a collection of humorous yet uplifting affirmations designed to boost the spirits of anyone knee-deep in GPSMF drama. Phrases like, "I believe in the goodness of people, but I also believe in background checks," or "I'm worth more than a last-minute 'U up?' text," can serve as daily reminders for readers navigating the tricky GPSMF terrain.

GPSMF Confessionals: Readers Share Their "Believing" Moments

Ah, belief – it's a powerful, sometimes delusional force that's caused many of us to think, say, or do things that in hindsight seem, well... absurd. In this fun section, readers (and a few fictional folks) share their cringe-worthy, facepalm-inducing moments of blind belief in their GPSMFs. It's all in good fun, so let's dive into these confessional tales!

1. Sarah, 28:
"I once believed my GPSMF when he said he didn't reply to my messages for three days because he was 'kidnapped by ninjas'. Instead of being alarmed, I was just impressed he escaped."

2. Mike, 32:
"My GPSMF once told me she couldn't make it to my brother's wedding because she was selected to be on a 'secret reality TV show'. I bragged about it to everyone. Turned out, she was just attending her ex's beach party."

3. Priya, 25:

"After hearing the same 'I lost my phone' excuse five times in one month, I actually believed him. I even bought him a new one! Later found out he had a collection at home – one for each girlfriend."

4. Lucas, 29:

"When my GPSMF told me she had a rare condition where she'd turn into a werewolf if she got too emotionally involved, I spent nights researching werewolf transformations online. I was ready to be her Jacob Black."

5. Tasha, 30:

"I believed him every time he said he was working late, only to find out his version of 'working late' was just late-night gaming sessions with his buddies."

6. Alex, 26:

"She told me she missed our date because she had to rush to the airport to stop her best friend from boarding a flight to join a circus. It seemed movie-like, and I believed it, until I saw her Instagram story at a local bar."

7. Felicia, 27:

"When he told me he was attending a 'whispering conference' where everyone only whispers, I spent days practicing my whispering skills to impress him. Only later did I find out he just had a weekend getaway."

There you have it! These confessional tales remind us that we're all human. We sometimes get swept up in stories, often because we want to believe the best about those we care about. While these anecdotes are light-hearted, they underscore an essential point: belief should be built on trust and reality, not just charming tales.

STEP 3
INVENTORY OF PERSONAL
RELATIONSHIP PATTERNS

Every closet has its hidden treasures and skeletons. In the expansive wardrobe of our hearts, there are relationship patterns that have woven themselves into the fabric of our romantic tales. Taking an inventory isn't about self-blame; it's a journey of understanding, recognition, and ultimately, growth.

The "Ex-files": Analyzing Past Relationships

Hannah, a spirited journalist in her mid-30s, recalls the day she sat down with a box of old letters, photos, and mementos – her 'ex-files'. As she sifted through, memories flooded back. She laughed at some old jokes, cringed at past mistakes, but most importantly, she noticed patterns. Each letter, each photo seemed to tell the same story, just with a different face.

Taking an analytical dive into your past relationships isn't about dwelling in nostalgia. It's about understanding where you've been to figure out where you're headed. Each relationship, however fleeting, has lessons that sculpt our future choices.

Spotting Recurring Themes: Are GPSMFs Your Relationship Kryptonite?

Just like Superman has his Kryptonite, some of us have our relationship Achilles' heel. For some, it might be the allure of the "bad boy" or the "mystery woman." For others, it might be someone who needs "saving."

Emma, a schoolteacher, admits, "I always felt drawn to men who seemed like they needed guidance, almost like my students. And every time, I'd end up feeling drained." Recognizing these recurring themes, these GPSMFs in your love narrative, is the first step in changing the narrative itself.

Tales from the Trenches: Relationship Blunders We've All Made

1. The "I Can Change Him" Saga: Lisa met Mark during a summer camp. He was the quintessential rebel - leather jacket, motorbike, and that air of mystery. Despite warnings from friends, Lisa believed she could be the one to 'change' him. Three years later, the only change was in Lisa's patience level.

2. The "Opposites Attract, Right?" Tale: Raj and Sophie came from two entirely different worlds. He loved classical music; she was a rock chick. While the initial thrill of discovering new worlds was exhilarating, they soon realized that opposites might attract, but they also frequently clash.

3. The "Let's Just Ignore That Red Flag" Chronicles: When Jamie noticed that his girlfriend, Clara, had a habit of brushing off his feelings, he chose to ignore it. It was just a minor flaw, right? Until the day he found himself feeling like a background character in his own relationship story.

Every relationship blunder, every misstep, is a chapter in our love journey. And while they might make for some cringeworthy memories, they are also the very tales that define us, that teach us, and that propel us towards a love story that's truly worth the read.

Concluding Thoughts:

Relationship patterns, whether delightful or daunting, are essential signposts on our path of love. By delving deep into our ex-files, recognizing our relationship kryptonites, and chuckling over our blunders, we equip ourselves to embrace a future that's not just a repeat of the past but a beautiful evolution.

STEP 4

DECIDE TO TURN OVER CONTROL

Linda sat across from her best friend, sipping her mocha latte, and said, "I just wish I had a remote to control his every move." Her friend raised an eyebrow and chuckled, "Like one of those universal remotes for TVs? Good luck with that!" But the sentiment behind Linda's wish is one that resonates with many - the desire to have control, especially when you see a loved one, like a GPSMF, making decisions you don't necessarily agree with.

Surrender vs. Submission: Know the Difference

It's an age-old conundrum in love. *Do I let go or hold on tighter?* Jane, a therapist with over 20 years of counseling couples, puts it succinctly: "It's the art of knowing when to steer the ship and when to let the currents take over." But don't mistake surrendering for submission. To submit is to lose oneself, to let another overshadow your essence. Surrender, on the other hand, is a conscious choice to trust the journey, understanding that you can't navigate every twist and turn.

The Myth of the 'Fixer-Upper'

Ah, the classic story. You meet someone, and instead of seeing them for who they are, you see a 'project.' Sarah, a 28-year-old accountant, recalls, "I met Jake during college. I thought I could change him, turn him from a party boy into husband material. I was wrong." Movies make it look so easy. The wild one gets tamed, the bad boy becomes good, but real life isn't a screenplay. Jake wasn't Sarah's project; he was her partner. And that required mutual effort, not unilateral 'fixing.'

Humor Highlight: The GPSMF Remote Control Fiasco

Imagine for a moment that you *did* get a universal remote to control your GPSMF. You sit gleefully on your couch, pointing and clicking. "Listen" makes him nod, "Apologize" elicits a baffled sorry, and "Clean" has him vacuuming in circles. But then, the batteries start to fade, the commands go haywire, and suddenly, he's dancing the cha-cha in your living room with no off button in sight. The moral? Control isn't all it's cracked up to be.

Empowerment: The Joy in Letting Go

Ask Maria, who after a tumultuous relationship with her GPSMF, found strength in vulnerability. "When I stopped trying to puppeteer every move, I found peace. Not just in our relationship, but within myself," she shared. Letting go doesn't signify weakness; it's a testament to your inner strength, your capacity to believe in life's unpredictable beauty.

The Role of Trust in Turning Over Control

Trust is the bedrock of any lasting relationship. And it isn't built in grand gestures but everyday moments. From letting him plan a surprise date to trusting him to handle a crisis, it's about the collective moments that form a mosaic of trust. But remember, trusting your partner doesn't mean turning a blind eye. It means believing in your combined strength, and when things seem shaky, always having faith in your foundation.

Concluding Thoughts:

The dance of love is intricate, filled with dips and twirls. And sometimes, the most profound connection is found when we release control and trust our partner to catch us. In the intricate ballet of relationships, allow the music of trust and understanding to guide your steps.

STEP 5
READY FOR CHANGE

In the ever-evolving world of relationships, one thing remains constant – change is inevitable. Whether you're navigating the turbulent waters of a GPSMF relationship or simply looking to grow alongside your partner, embracing change is paramount. But as with any journey, this too starts from within.

The Mirror Moment: Looking Inwards Before Pointing Outwards

We've all been there. In the midst of an argument or a heated discussion, it's easy to play the blame game. But real growth begins when we pause, look in the mirror, and reflect on our role in the relationship dynamic.

Lucas, a marketing executive, shares a defining moment in his relationship. "I was always quick to point out my partner's shortcomings. One day, amidst a particularly intense disagreement, I caught a glimpse of myself in a mirror. The reflection of my red, angry face was a wake-up call. I realized I needed to address my own issues before pointing fingers."

Before seeking change in others, it's essential to be open to self-change. This might mean acknowledging personal flaws, recognizing harmful patterns, or even seeking professional help. Because ultimately, a relationship involves two individuals, and positive change requires effort from both sides.

The Evolution of a GPSMF Relationship: What Positive Change Looks Like

Change, especially in the context of a GPSMF relationship, isn't about a complete personality overhaul. It's about evolution, growth, and mutual respect.

Consider Jade and Alex. When Jade met Alex, he was the poster child for GPSMF behavior. But instead of giving up, Jade communicated her feelings. Over time, Alex began understanding the effects of his actions. He started attending therapy, began opening up about past traumas, and together, they forged a path of mutual growth.

This evolution doesn't mean Alex shed his GPSMF title overnight. It signifies that with understanding, patience, and effort, a GPSMF relationship can evolve into one of mutual respect and love.

Humorous Hiccups: When Trying to Change Takes a Funny Turn

1. The Yoga Misadventure: Sarah wanted her partner, Mike, to embrace a healthier lifestyle. So, she enrolled both of them in a yoga class. On day one, Mike, in an attempt to master the 'Downward Dog', ended up causing a domino effect, toppling three fellow participants. They never returned to that class, but the memory always elicited hearty laughter.

2. The Failed Vegan Week: To improve their diet, Robert decided he and his girlfriend would go vegan for a week. By day three, his girlfriend caught him sneaking a cheeseburger at midnight. They both laughed it off and decided that perhaps a balanced diet was more their speed.

3. DIY Relationship Counseling: After reading a self-help book, Emily decided to have a 'relationship feedback session' with her boyfriend, Tom. Equipped with a whiteboard and markers, she started listing pros and cons. An hour later, the board was full of doodles, jokes, and a plan for their next vacation.

Change can be challenging, intimidating, and sometimes downright hilarious. But at its core, it's a testament to the human spirit's resilience and the lengths we'll go to, for love and personal growth.

STEP 6
SETTING BOUNDARIES

Navigating the unpredictable seas of a relationship with a GPSMF requires a sturdy ship and an even sturdier compass: boundaries. But how do you lay down the rules without sounding like a dictator? And is there room for humor amidst the seriousness? As always, the journey is as important as the destination.

The Blueprint of Healthy Boundaries in a Relationship

Imagine building a house without a blueprint. The results would be chaotic, at best. Similarly, without clear boundaries, a relationship can quickly devolve into a maze of confusion and resentment.

Establishing healthy boundaries means understanding and respecting personal and shared spaces, both physically and emotionally. It means knowing when to step in and when to step back. It's a dialogue that both partners participate in, resulting in a relationship where both feel safe, respected, and cherished.

Emma, a relationship therapist, emphasizes, "Setting boundaries isn't about restricting the other person; it's about creating a safe environment where both partners can flourish."

The Tightrope Walk: Being Firm without Being Unfair

Boundaries can sometimes be misconstrued as barriers, especially in a GPSMF relationship. Striking the right balance is crucial.

Take Maya and Leo, for example. Maya wanted personal time every evening to unwind with a book. Leo, a quintessential GPSMF, saw this as her pushing him away. After several discussions, they found a middle ground: Maya would have her quiet reading time, while Leo used that period for his hobbies. This compromise allowed them both personal space without feeling isolated.

Being firm about boundaries doesn't mean being rigid. It means understanding the essence of the boundary and being flexible in its application.

Comical Moments: When Setting Boundaries Got Absurd

1. The Cookie Jar Incident: Rachel set a boundary that her special cookie jar was off-limits to Jake, her sweet-toothed boyfriend. One evening, she found him with cookie crumbs all over his face, claiming a cookie fairy must've visited. They laughed it off, but the cookie jar now sits on a higher shelf.

2. The Bathroom Ballad: Josh and Tina decided to set boundaries around morning routines. Josh was to stay out of the bathroom while Tina did her makeup. The next day, Josh serenaded her from outside the bathroom door, turning a boundary-setting moment into a hilarious musical morning.

3. The "No TV" Pact: Emily and Sam set a boundary to have no TV nights to enhance their communication. One evening, Emily caught Sam sneaking glances at a muted TV through reflections on their fish tank. The two burst out laughing, realizing that sometimes, rules are meant to be creatively bent.

Setting boundaries, while crucial, needn't always be a somber affair. With understanding, communication, and a dash of humor, they can become the pillars of a strong, loving relationship.

STEP 7
SEEK HUMILITY

In the dance of relationships, sometimes we're the ones stepping on toes. Recognizing our imperfections and letting go of the innate desire to always be right can shift dynamics like nothing else, especially when tangoing with a GPSMF. Humility, when combined with self-awareness and humor, can be the unexpected relationship salve we've all been looking for.

Understanding We're All Flawed

No one, not even the person staring back at you from the mirror, is perfect. We've all made mistakes, misunderstood situations, and acted irrationally. Recognizing these imperfections is the first step toward embracing them. It's not about tearing ourselves down, but about understanding that we're all works in progress.

Dr. Lina James, a renowned relationship coach, says, "True strength lies in acknowledging our weaknesses. In vulnerability, we find connections deeper than we ever imagined."

Navigating the Ego: Yours, Mine, and Ours

Egos can be demanding, throwing tantrums when they feel bruised or ignored. In a relationship, it's a constant balancing act between three entities: your ego, your partner's, and the combined ego of the relationship itself.

Remember, it's not about crushing or ignoring the ego, but

rather learning to navigate it. Sometimes it means swallowing pride and admitting wrong, sometimes it's about standing up for oneself, and sometimes it's about laughing at how absurdly large our egos can puff themselves up to be.

Light-hearted Tales of Times We Weren't the Heroes

1. The Great Spaghetti Standoff: Sarah was sure her spaghetti sauce was the best. One dinner, she argued with her partner, Tim, who believed his grandmother's recipe reigned supreme. Neither would back down, and what was supposed to be a romantic dinner turned into a spaghetti standoff. A week later, they held a blind taste test with friends, and it turned out... neither of their sauces won. They now laugh about the "Great Sauce Scandal" at every dinner party.

2. The "Shortcut" that Wasn't: Mark was convinced he knew the best shortcut on their road trip. Despite Lisa's reservations and the GPS's clear directions, he took his "shortcut" - leading them on a 2-hour detour. Instead of gloating, Lisa just played "Lost Highway" on the car stereo, making them both chuckle.

3. The Mystery of the Missing Keys: Ana always chastised Roberto for misplacing things. One day, after a long lecture on "being more attentive", she realized she had misplaced her keys. The irony wasn't lost on Roberto, who teased her by turning it into a dramatic detective quest around the house. They found the keys... in Ana's bag.

Seeking humility is about embracing the imperfections and understanding that they contribute as much to the fabric of our relationships as our strengths. After all, perfection is overrated; it's the quirks, blunders, and laughter that make memories.

STEP 8
LIST OF AFFECTED RELATIONSHIPS

GPSMF dynamics aren't isolated incidents, confined to the borders of that one relationship. The waves they produce often ripple out, touching family, friends, and sometimes even work colleagues. This chapter delves into the widespread impact of GPSMF relationships, the art of mending what's broken, and finding the lighter moments within the chaos.

The Ripple Effect: When GPSMF Dynamics Affect Other Relationships

Like a stone tossed into a still pond, the dynamics of a tumultuous relationship can send ripples far and wide. Parents worry when they see their children unhappy, friends feel the strain when they're constantly providing a shoulder to cry on or being put in the middle, and siblings often bear the brunt of the venting sessions.

There's no "clean" breakup or dispute in the world of GPSMF. The drama, the highs, and lows, the uncertainty — they don't stay neatly tucked into one corner of our lives. They spill over, leaving many others wet in the process.

Rebuilding Bridges: Moving Forward after Missteps

One of the biggest realizations GPSMF survivors come to is recognizing the collateral damage. When you're in the eye of the storm, it's hard to see the wider devastation. But in the calm that follows, the view becomes painfully clear.

1. **Open Dialogue:** Talking is healing. Addressing the elephant in the room with those who've been affected is the first step towards rebuilding. Whether it's apologizing, explaining, or simply listening, opening a channel of communication is crucial.

2. **Actively Reinvest:** Making amends isn't just about saying sorry. It's about showing through actions that things have changed. Whether it's setting boundaries, seeking therapy, or creating healthier habits, your loved ones need to see the change to believe in it.

3. **Let Time Heal:** Some relationships might not mend immediately. And that's okay. Give it time. Keep showing up, keep trying, and eventually, bridges will begin to mend.

Laugh Break: That Time When...

1. **The Forgotten Anniversary:** Emily was so wrapped up in the latest GPSMF drama that she forgot her parents' 30th wedding anniversary. On realizing her oversight, she sent them a hilarious card that read, "Sorry I missed the big day, I was busy saving a sinking ship. Happy 30-ish Anniversary!"

2. **Double Booked Dates:** Jake, in a bid to keep his GPSMF away from a family gathering, told him the wrong date. Unfortunately, he also forgot to inform his sister, resulting in two surprise guests on two different days. His family now teases him about his "double booking" skills every holiday.

3. **The Accidental Group Text:** Lily meant to send a venting message about her GPSMF to her best friend. Instead, she sent it to a group that included him. The group name? "Sunday Brunch Crew." They all laugh about it now, especially when deciding on brunch venues.

Recognizing the wider impact of our GPSMF adventures isn't about wallowing in guilt. It's about understanding, taking responsibility, and moving forward with lessons learned. And, as with everything in life, a dash of humor can make the journey a bit more bearable.

STEP 9

MAKE AMENDS WHERE POSSIBLE

In the realm of relationships, particularly those that are tumultuous, we're bound to step on some toes, either inadvertently or otherwise. But healing, both personal and relational, often requires us to turn back, recognize our missteps, and where possible, extend an olive branch. This chapter focuses on the transformative power of making amends, not just for those we've hurt, but for our own peace of mind and personal growth.

Echoes of the Past: Recognizing the Hurt

Before making amends, there's a crucial step many overlook: truly understanding the nature and extent of the pain we might have caused. Every relationship has its dynamics, and in the whirlwind of GPSMF, there's collateral damage, sometimes to people we never intended to hurt.

Imagine past relationships as rooms in a long corridor. Some doors might be slightly ajar, with memories slipping through, while others might be locked tight. Now's the time to walk that corridor and gently push open those doors. What do you see? What feelings resurface?

Reaching Out: The Art of Making Amends

Making amends isn't just a simple "I'm sorry." It's an art that requires sincerity, vulnerability, and a genuine desire to set things right.

1. Self Reflection: Before reaching out, understand why you want to make amends. Is it for closure? To rebuild the relationship? Knowing your "why" will guide the conversation.

2. Choosing the Right Time and Place: Timing matters. If it's been years, understand that the other person might have moved on, or the hurt might still be fresh. Choose a setting that's neutral and comfortable for both.

3. Listening: Making amends isn't a monologue. It's a dialogue. Listen to their side, their feelings, and their perspective.

4. Accepting Responses: Not everyone will be ready to accept your amends. And that's okay. The gesture, if genuine, is a step towards healing, regardless of the outcome.

Stories from the Heart: When Making Amends Made a Difference

1. Sarah & The Lost Friendship: Sarah's relationship with a GPSMF had isolated her from her closest friend, Lisa. They went years without speaking. One day, Sarah reached out, not expecting much. Today, they're closer than ever, often joking about the "lost years."

2. Tom's Family Reunion: Tom's family had always been close-knit until his tumultuous relationship began causing rifts. After it ended, he organized a family reunion, using it as a platform to apologize and reconnect. It was an emotional, cathartic evening, marking the start of a new chapter for the entire family.

3. Nina's Letter: Unable to face her ex after realizing her mistakes, Nina wrote a heartfelt letter. She poured out her regrets, her wishes, and her apologies. A week later, she received a postcard: "Thank you. Wishing you peace."

Making amends is more than a gesture; it's a journey. A journey of understanding, of growth, and ultimately, of healing. While not all paths will lead to reconciliation, every step taken with genuine intent is a step towards personal redemption.

STEP 10
CONTINUE PERSONAL INVENTORY

Self-awareness is a continual process, akin to a gardener tending to their garden. While planting the seeds of change is essential, the real work lies in the meticulous care, the vigilant watch for weeds, and the ability to adapt as the seasons change. This chapter emphasizes the need to regularly introspect and adjust our relationship dynamics and personal patterns to ensure growth and harmony.

The Power of Self-Check-ins

The landscape of our mind, feelings, and behaviors is ever-changing. To navigate this dynamic terrain, one needs to periodically stop, assess, and recalibrate.

1. Scheduled Introspections: Set aside dedicated time every week or month to reflect upon your actions, reactions, and feelings. Journaling can be a powerful tool here, creating a record to look back on.

2. Feedback Loops: Surround yourself with people who care about you and aren't afraid to offer candid feedback. Sometimes, an outsider's perspective can highlight blind spots.

3. The Alarm Bells: Recognize your triggers. If you find yourself slipping into old patterns, have mechanisms in place to pull yourself back. This could be a mantra, a confidant, or a particular ritual.

Adjusting Your Compass: Adapting to Change

Growth isn't linear. We all face setbacks. The key is to adjust our approach based on these experiences.

1. Celebrate Small Victories: Every time you identify an old pattern and choose differently, take a moment to recognize and celebrate it.

2. Embrace Failures as Lessons: Rather than beating yourself up over relapses, ask: What can I learn from this? How can I ensure it doesn't happen again?

3. Seek External Resources: Books, counseling, or group discussions can offer new perspectives and tools to aid your journey.

Anecdotes from the Road Less Traveled

1. Anna's Alarm Bell: Anna had a unique method to pull herself out of spirals. She'd wear a rubber band on her wrist and snap it whenever she recognized an old pattern surfacing. It was her tactile reminder to choose differently.

2. Raj's Monthly Retreat: Once a month, Raj would go to his favorite spot in the park, armed with a notebook. He'd spend hours reflecting, writing, and setting intentions for the next month. It was his ritual of grounding and growth.

3. Lia and Her Mirror Conversations: Every morning, Lia would talk to herself in the mirror, discussing her feelings, applauding her progress, and addressing her shortcomings. It was her way of beginning each day with self-awareness.

In the end, the path to personal growth and harmonious relationships is not set in stone. It winds and twists, presenting both challenges and rewards. By continuing personal inventory, we arm ourselves with the insights and adaptability to walk this path with grace, resilience, and an ever-evolving understanding of ourselves and those we cherish.

STEP 11
SEEK GROWTH

The journey to self-awareness and relationship harmony doesn't end at realization; it's a never-ending quest for improvement. Growth is the compass that guides us forward, ensuring that we do not stagnate or revert to old patterns. This chapter dives deep into the various avenues one can explore to foster growth, both individually and in relationships.

The Pillars of Personal Growth

Growth is multidimensional, arising from various facets of our lives. Tapping into different sources allows us to develop a holistic perspective.

1. **Therapeutic Avenues:** Engaging with a professional therapist can provide tailored insights and coping mechanisms. Their expertise offers a structured approach to navigating personal and relationship challenges.

2. **Literary Exploration:** Books serve as windows to the world and mirrors reflecting our souls. Whether it's self-help books, autobiographies, or fiction, literature can impart invaluable life lessons.

3. **Meditative Practices:** Mindfulness and meditation anchor us to the present and cultivate inner peace. Regular practice can improve emotional regulation, understanding, and compassion.

4. **Wise Council:** Trusted friends and family offer both support and constructive feedback. Their experiences and perspectives

can shine a light on areas we might overlook.

Tools for the Journey

To seek growth is to arm oneself with tools and strategies that ensure forward momentum.

1. Personal Growth Plans: Outline your growth goals, be it emotional intelligence, better communication, or patience. Break them down into actionable steps and periodically assess your progress.

2. Growth Retreats: Taking a break from the hustle and bustle of daily life to focus solely on personal development can be transformative. This could be a solo trip, a workshop, or a retreat centered around growth.

3. Digital Resources: The online realm is a treasure trove of courses, webinars, and forums dedicated to personal growth and relationship betterment. Make the most of them.

Stories of Transformation

1. Jake's Book Club: Jake started a monthly book club focused solely on personal development books. Not only did he gain insights from the books, but the diverse interpretations of his club members added layers to his understanding.

2. Mia's Meditation Retreat: A weekend retreat transformed Mia's life. The silence, the introspection, and the guided sessions gave her clarity she had never experienced before.

3. Carlos and Aunt Clara: Every Sunday, Carlos would spend an hour talking to his Aunt Clara, a lady who had seen the ups and downs of life. Her wisdom, advice, and anecdotes were his guideposts.

Embarking on the path to growth requires commitment, effort, and patience. But the rewards — enhanced self-awareness, improved relationships, and a deeper understanding of life's tapestry — are well worth the journey. Remember, growth isn't about perfection; it's about progress, one step at a time.

STEP 12

SPREAD THE KNOWLEDGE

"In learning you will teach, and in teaching you will learn."
– Phil Collins

The culmination of this journey isn't just personal enlightenment but also the ripple effect that it can create. When you've navigated the stormy seas of complex relationship dynamics and reached calmer shores, extending a helping hand to others can be the most rewarding experience.

Why Sharing is Caring

1. Perspective: As you teach, you'll encounter diverse experiences and perspectives that can further broaden your own view. It's a cycle of perpetual learning.

2. Solidification: Sharing what you've learned reinforces your own knowledge. It helps to root your experiences deeper, making your understanding robust.

3. Empathy: Teaching others allows you to walk a mile in someone else's shoes, fostering a profound sense of empathy and connection.

How to Pass the Torch

1. Start Conversations: Casual discussions with friends or acquaintances can be enlightening. Share your journey, listen to theirs, and find common ground.

2. Host Workshops: Organize or participate in workshops that focus on relationships and personal growth. These structured settings allow for deeper dives into subjects.

3. Blogging or Vlogging: Sharing your experiences online can reach a wider audience. Write articles, create videos, or even start a podcast.

4. Support Groups: Join or create support groups where individuals can share experiences, support each other, and learn together.

5. Mentorship: Take someone under your wing. One-on-one mentoring can be a deeply rewarding way to share insights and experiences.

Anecdotes of Spreading the Seeds of Knowledge

1. Sarah's Saturday Sessions: Every Saturday, Sarah invited a small group to her home for a discussion on relationship dynamics. These sessions became a sanctuary for many.

2. Raj's Relationship Blog: Raj started blogging about his experiences. What began as a therapeutic outlet soon became a beacon for many seeking guidance.

3. Anna and the Local Library: Anna organized bi-monthly talks at her local library, inviting experts and novices alike to share their tales and techniques.

In the end, it's about creating a community of understanding, support, and growth. As you light the path for others, your own way becomes clearer. The journey of navigating complex relationships doesn't end with self-realization; it's an ongoing process of growth, sharing, and mutual upliftment.

STEP 13
CONCLUSION

The Unlucky Step 13: From GPSMF Chaos to Relationship Clarity

Ah, Step 13. An intentional nod to the superstitions surrounding the number. In many cultures, 13 is considered unlucky, but here, it serves as a stark reminder. It's the wake-up call to say, "Have we truly learned? Or are we doomed to repeat past mistakes?" You see, there's no actual 13th step in our program, but there's a world outside this book where actions speak louder than words. If we keep stumbling into the same GPSMF-laden pitfalls, we may very well be crafting our Step 13 – an endless loop of chaotic encounters.

The path we've traversed thus far wasn't always smooth. At times, it felt like we were trying to find our way out of a perplexing maze. However, step by step, through admittance, reflection, boundary-setting, seeking humility, and more, we've made progress.

From GPSMF Chaos to Relationship Clarity: The Journey So Far

When we began this voyage, we embarked not just on an exploration of relationship dynamics, but also of self-awareness, growth, and understanding. The path wasn't always smooth, and at times it felt like we were navigating a maze with no exit. Yet, step by step, through admittance, reflection, boundary-setting, seeking humility, and more, we moved closer to clarity.

The very idea of the GPSMF is an embodiment of our society's relationship pitfalls. These characters, as we've come to understand, are not inherently villains in our tales but often products of various circumstances, both personal and societal. Their behavior, while challenging, offers a mirror to our own vulnerabilities, desires, and fears.

The truth we must reckon with is that GPSMFs aren't just external entities; their shadows often lurk within us. This journey was never about changing others; it was about understanding and transforming ourselves, deciphering our patterns, and forging a path toward healthier relationships.

Embracing the Future, GPSMFs and All

As we close this book, it's essential to recognize that our journey is far from over. Relationships, by nature, are dynamic. They evolve, just as we do. Our experiences with GPSMFs have provided invaluable lessons, but they are just one chapter in our intricate relationship story.

The future might hold encounters with more GPSMFs, but equipped with the knowledge, insight, and tools you've gained, you're better prepared to navigate those challenges. Remember, every relationship, no matter how tumultuous, offers an opportunity for growth.

Spread your knowledge, lean on your support systems, and never stop seeking personal growth. There's a world full of relationships out there, each unique and valuable in its own right. Embrace them, GPSMFs and all, and continue writing your unique story of love, understanding, and evolution.

Remember, life isn't about avoiding the storms; it's about learning to dance in the rain.

Thank you for joining this journey. May your path be filled with understanding, growth, love, and the wisdom to navigate the challenges that come your way.

ABOUT THE AUTHOR

Emmanuel Simms: CEO of In Vivo Exposure & Author of "The Rules of a Successful Failure"

Emmanuel Simms isn't just an entrepreneur; he's a beacon of hope and inspiration. As the mastermind behind In Vivo Exposure, he champions the bold philosophy of confronting fears head-on. His innovative platform is a testament to his commitment to pushing the boundaries of human potential, allowing individuals to break free from anxieties and embrace life's myriad opportunities with zeal.

The scope of Emmanuel's influence extends far beyond his groundbreaking platform. He's also a renowned author, captivating readers with his book, "The Rules of a Successful Failure." Through its pages, Emmanuel provides a raw, unfiltered look into embracing setbacks, channeling them into lessons, and ultimately converting failures into stepping stones to success.

Emmanuel's keen insights on personal growth, combined with his unparalleled understanding of human capability, has ignited a spark in readers across the globe. They've been enthralled, motivated, and emboldened to face challenges, chase dreams, and carve paths to greatness. It's no wonder he's emerged as a highly sought-after speaker and mentor, especially in the arenas of self-improvement and entrepreneurial spirit.

His magnetic charisma, combined with poignant teachings and evocative narratives, have solidified Emmanuel's reputation as a transformative figure. For those who yearn for profound change, success in their endeavors, or a renaissance in their personal and professional spheres, Emmanuel Simms offers the beacon light.

Dive deep into his ethos, be captivated by "The Rules of a Successful Failure," and allow Emmanuel to guide you towards a journey of growth, resilience, and unparalleled success. Embrace his vision, and let your trajectory be forever uplifted.

Join the movement. Immerse yourself in the wisdom of Emmanuel Simms. #InVivoExposure #Author #TransformationalSpeaker #EudaimoniaHealers

Made in the USA
Middletown, DE
22 October 2023